Surviving Drug

By Paul Mason
Real Life Heroes
Series of 6
Arcturus Publishing Imprint
978-1-84837-691-5
$32.80 (List)/$22.95 (School/Library) each
48 Pages
Reading Level: Grade 6 and up
Color photographs, Case studies with first-person accounts, sidebars
Release Date: September, 2010
LOC: 2010014146

This dynamic series provides an inside look at the courage and heroism real-life children have shown in battling illness and overcoming difficult circumstances. Each volume begins with an introduction to the topic, followed by ten different true-life stories. Sidebars explaining additional details accompany these personal accounts to further flesh out the topic.

Why did we publish this series?
These volumes provide the reader with real-life stories so compelling that they might think they're reading a TV script, bringing students an understanding that cold hard facts alone can't easily deliver. The books also include informative background information, making the volumes valuable for supplementing a variety of curriculums, sparking classroom discussions, and providing sources for reports & projects.

Real Life Heroes
Other titles in this series:
Asylum Seekers
Surviving Cancer
Surviving Gangs and Bullying
Surviving HIV/AIDS
Surviving Natural Disasters

Contact Information:
Ann Schwab
aschwab@blackrabbitbooks.com
507.388.1633

REAL LIFE HEROES

SURVIVING DRUG ADDICTION

REAL LIFE HEROES

SURVIVING DRUG ADDICTION

Paul Mason

ARCTURUS

Introduction

What are drugs? Drugs are substances which, when taken into the body, change the way it works. Some drugs change the chemical balance of the brain. For example, they may trigger the release of the chemical dopamine, which leads to feelings of happiness. Some drugs affect the functioning of the body. They speed up a person's heartbeat, for instance. Some drugs affect both the mind and the body.

Using drugs

Drugs are often used for medical purposes. For example, ephedrine is a decongestant drug used in today's cold cures. People also use drugs for pleasure. Among the most popular pleasure drugs are alcohol and tobacco. Both of these are legal in many countries, but other pleasure drugs are illegal. These are often called street drugs. Ephedrine, for example, has a pleasure-drug use. It can be used to make another drug, called methamphetamine, which produces feelings of intense pleasure.

Different types of drug

Drugs can be divided into three main categories, based on their effects: stimulants, depressants, and psychoactive drugs.

- stimulants speed up the body's functions. They make your heart beat faster, increase your blood pressure, and make you feel more alert and lively. Popular stimulants include cocaine, amphetamines, caffeine (in coffee and tea), and nicotine (in cigarettes).
- depressants slow down the body's functions. They slow down your heart rate, you breathe more slowly, and you feel more relaxed. Your speech can become slurred and you can lose coordination. Popular depressants include alcohol, GHB, heroin, and sleeping pills.
- Psychoactive drugs affect the way people see, hear,

◀ The white powder is heroin and the red pills are metamphetamines. They have been seized by police in Thailand in a crackdown on illegal drugs. Part of Thailand, called the Golden Triangle, is famous for growing opium, from which heroin is made.

▶ This woman in China is a heroin addict, and also has HIV/AIDS. This deadly disease is more common among heroin addicts than other people because they share needles to inject the drug. The used needle carries the disease from one addict to the next.

and feel. They may cause people to sense things that are not, in fact, there. Popular psychoactive drugs include LSD, MDMA (which is found in ecstasy), and ketamine.

Some drugs combine more than one of these: cannabis, for example, is both a depressant and a psychoactive drug. Ecstasy is a psychoactive drug, but is often cut, or mixed in, with the stimulant speed.

Drug addiction

People who take drugs regularly risk becoming addicted—they come to depend on the drug so strongly that they believe they cannot live without it. People who start taking drugs do not plan to become addicts. But their need for drugs grows more powerful until it is the most important thing in their lives. Everything else—family, friends, and work—comes second to their need for drugs.

Top ten most dangerous drugs

In 2007 a British study tried to work out which ten drugs were the most dangerous. The study used three measures for working out how dangerous a drug was: the harm it did to the user, its addictiveness, and its impact on society. This was their conclusion (1 being the most dangerous and 10 being the least):
1. Heroin
2. Cocaine
3. Barbiturates
4. Street methadone
5. Alcohol
6. Ketamine
7. Benzodiazepine
8. Amphetamine
9. Tobacco
10. Buprenorphine

Cannabis came in at 11, LSD at 14, and ecstasy at 18.

Source: *The Lancet*, March 2007

▶ **This young woman in San Francisco, California, is suffering from withdrawal, the physical effects of trying to stop taking drugs. Her joints are aching and she feels feverish, and she thinks that only drugs will make her feel well again.**

Drug addiction and health

Drug addiction can affect the user's health in different ways, depending on the drug:

- Some drugs—ketamine, LSD, and skunk cannabis, for example—have been associated with mental illnesses.
- Alcohol can cause liver disease, heart problems, cancer, and brain damage.
- Many drugs carry a risk of overdose. Overdose occurs when the drug's effect is so strong that the body shuts down, causing severe illness or death.
- Drugs that are injected, such as heroin, carry the risk of infection by deadly diseases such as HIV and hepatitis B. This is because the users sometimes share needles and the disease is passed from one person to the next in the needle.
- Drugs often cause people to lose their inhibitions and act in ways they would not normally consider. This can include violence or reckless sexual behavior (making drug takers more likely to fall prey to sexually transmitted diseases).

Drugs and families

Drug addiction affects the families of addicts as well as the addicts themselves. As the stories in this book show, drug addicts sometimes steal from their parents, neglect their children, or abuse their husband or wife because of their need for drugs.

The cost of drugs

Drugs are expensive, and few addicts have enough money of their own to pay for the drugs they need. Many become involved in crime, including robbery, burglary, shoplifting, and prostitution, as a way of paying for their drugs.

Drugs cost money in other ways, too. Governments spend huge sums each year on law enforcement, the justice system, and prisons to deal with drug-related crime.

The treatments addicts need cost health services huge sums of money each year. All of this must be paid for by taxes.

Escaping drug addiction

Given the harm they do to other people and society in general, it is tempting to think that drug addicts deserve no sympathy. But no one who tries a drug for the first time is planning to become an addict. Those who do become addicted to drugs are trapped in a world where the drug takes over their lives. Escaping takes hard work and dedication, and many addicts fail.

This book tells the stories of young people directly affected by drug addiction, the difficulties they have encountered and how they have survived. The stories are all true, but people's names and some aspects of their identity have been changed.

A deadly habit

• Worldwide, 20–24 million people are addicted to illegal drugs.

• Roughly 200,000 people die each year as a result of taking illegal drugs.

• Nearly two million die as a result of alcohol abuse.

• Five million die as a result of smoking cigarettes.

Source: United Nations World Drug Report, 2009

▼ **The man in the car is buying street drugs in a small plastic bag. Until he tries them, he cannot be sure what the bag contains or what other substances the drugs have been mixed with.**

Bill's world finally began to go to pieces when he got hooked on methamphetamine. "Meth" is a psychostimulant, which gives users a feeling of intense pleasure. But the "comedown" as the drug leaves their system can be very unpleasant. Users feel depressed and anxious and crave drugs—particularly more meth. In comparison with the meth high, events that people would normally find pleasurable begin to seem dull and uninteresting.

Methamphetamine

Methamphetamine is a highly addictive drug. There are several different names for methamphetamine, including meth, crank, ice, and crystal. One sign that someone is using the drug is "meth mouth": rotten teeth that eventually fall out. Users very quickly develop a physical and psychological reliance on the drug, and are only able to feel happy when taking it.

Bill had always been careful not to take drugs at home. But his meth addiction made him much less cautious. His mom walked into his room as he was in the process of sniffing speed, a stimulant, before heading off to his Saturday job. Bill barged past her and left, but when he got home that night his mom and dad were waiting for him. They put Bill into a

▼ Methamphetamine powder in a foil wrapper. Taking "meth" leads the brain to release dopamine, causing tremendous happiness. Once the drug wears off, the happiness is replaced by a feeling of emptiness, which only more meth can end.

▲ A British man is arrested in Bali, Indonesia, after being caught with methamphetamine. Like many countries, Indonesia has strict punishments for people found guilty of selling drugs.

rehab (rehabilitation) center, where he spent the next three weeks. But when he got out, Bill quickly slid back into his old ways. His mom knew what he was up to, but couldn't find a way of stopping him.

Bill had been stealing to pay for drugs for years, but had never been caught. When the police did finally catch up with him, it was for a traffic offense. The officer searched Bill's car and discovered all kinds of drug material: a glass pipe for smoking drugs, some speed, a small mirror, and credit card for chopping drugs up fine enough to sniff, and "baggies" — small, clear plastic bags for keeping drugs in. Bill was handcuffed and put in the back of the police car, arrested, and charged. Finally, in the cells at the police station, the reality of the situation hit Bill. It wasn't a game: he could be going to jail.

Bill's mom managed to get him released on bail the next day. He immediately asked her to help him get treatment for his addiction. By the end of the week he had signed up for a six-month course of drug counseling. Since the course ended Bill has not taken any kind of drug, even legal drugs such as alcohol. He now has a job, a girlfriend, and hope for a brighter future. As Bill admits, "I don't really want to think about how many brain cells I've lost—a lot. I wish I'd never smoked that first joint. But now my life has improved a hundred per cent."

Anders' Story

Anders lives in Denmark. He started taking drugs because he felt they might make him more successful at school and more entertaining in social situations. Soon he became an addict. It took Anders ten years to kick his drug habit and start to live a normal life. Today, though, he uses his terrible experiences to help other people avoid making the same mistakes he did.

Throughout his childhood Anders thought his parents were not interested in him. As he grew older he developed a very negative attitude. He was angry that his life was not going better, jealous of people who seemed more successful than him, and depressed at the thought that things would never improve. Most of all he felt constantly afraid—of what, he was not sure.

Things changed for Anders when he discovered alcohol and drugs. Unfortunately they did not change for the better. At first, when Anders was afraid, alcohol took away his fear. When he was angry, smoking cannabis calmed him down. Soon he began using a wide variety of drugs to change his moods. It was not long before Anders could no longer tell what he was really feeling. If he was paranoid, was he *really* paranoid, or was it the after effects of smoking cannabis? When he felt invincible, was he *really* confident, or was it because he had been sniffing cocaine? Anders' negative feelings returned, stronger than ever.

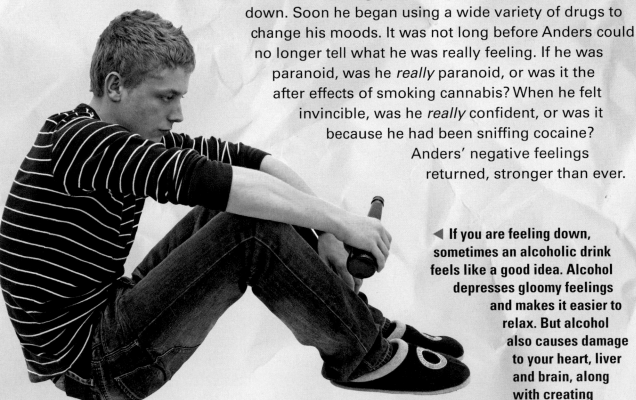

◄ If you are feeling down, sometimes an alcoholic drink feels like a good idea. Alcohol depresses gloomy feelings and makes it easier to relax. But alcohol also causes damage to your heart, liver and brain, along with creating other problems.

▲ People trying to beat their drug addiction attend a therapy session. Many addicts find that hearing about other people's battles with drugs, and speaking about their own, helps them to beat their addiction.

After ten years as an addict, Anders realized that if he did not stop taking drugs, they would kill him. As he says now, "I could not imagine life without drugs—but I found it even harder to imagine being dead!" He began to go to group counseling sessions. He met with other addicts at Alcoholics Anonymous and Narcotics Anonymous. Anders' counselor helped him see that drugs were making his problems worse, not better.

Group therapy

Group therapy is one of the most common ways of helping people get themselves off drugs and stay off drugs. A counselor leads the group: his or her role is to get people talking about their actions. Together, the group will discuss things such as:

- why members started taking drugs

- the actions their drug addiction caused them to take

- how drug addiction has affected their lives and the lives of people around them

- the challenges they face in trying to stay off drugs

Inspired by the example of his counselor, Anders decided to become one himself. As soon as he had been drug-free for a year, he began training to help other people get themselves off drugs and alcohol. He now works with drug addicts and alcoholics in the city of Odense. Anders says his recovery from addiction has been tough, but he now gets a great reward from helping others start the same journey to a drug-free life.

Amy's Story

Amy lives in Hastings on the south coast of England. She started using drugs at the age of 11. Amy's story is unusual because of how she got into drugs in the first place. She didn't have to worry about her parents discovering that she was developing a drug habit—they already knew. It was her father who gave Amy her first taste of cannabis.

Amy spent her childhood surrounded by drugs. Her father sold drugs from their house, so there were always addicts around. Amy's father enjoyed super-strength beer and skunk cannabis, but many of his friends and customers were heroin addicts. He would let them shoot up (inject themselves) in the bathroom, then lie around the house until the effect of the drug had worn away.

Amy first tried drugs when she was 11. She sniffed glue, and soon afterwards was given her first cannabis cigarette by her father. By the time she was a teenager Amy had moved on to smoking crack cocaine. It would be over 20 years before Amy would be able to rid herself of her addiction to crack.

Amy had children of her own when she was quite young. She used money that was meant to pay for the children's clothes and food, to pay for drugs. Amy went on to have six children, and all of them were affected by her drug addiction. She paid them little attention and her three youngest children were so badly looked after that they were taken into the foster care system.

▶ Tiny containers hold 'rocks' of crack. Behind them is a glass pipe, the kind that many addicts use to smoke the drug.

▶ "At this shelter there is hope," says this young drug addict. She has come to a shelter for drug addicts in Tulsa, Oklahoma. She hopes it will help her make a better life for herself and her baby daughter.

Many people would say that with a childhood like hers, it was inevitable that Amy would become hooked on drugs. Even so, in her 30s, she realized that drugs were ruining her life, and her children's. She underwent drug counseling. Amy had had counseling before but, as she says, "This time I was determined it would succeed." She finally managed to get herself drug-free, but her drug addiction had left a terrible legacy. Her three youngest children have never lived with her, and one of her older children is now a drug user herself.

Drug use and families

In 2009 a UK survey into the ways in which drug use by parents affect their children discovered the following:

- Some children had tried heroin at 12 or 13 as a result of being offered it by their mother or father.

- By the time they were between 10 and 14, a quarter of the children of drug addicts had tried drugs or alcohol.

- Between 15 and 17 years old, over half of the children had started habitually using drugs or alcohol.

- Many of the children said they had started taking drugs because it was the only way they could feel closer to their parents, who were otherwise not interested in them.

Source: UK Department of Health, reported in the *Guardian*, 14 January 2009

Tonya's Story

Ayear ago, Tonya's life was going nowhere fast. She had been a drug addict since she was 15. Having started with cannabis, she ended up taking heroin regularly, going out to buy ten-dollar bags on the street corners of Baltimore, Maryland. Today, though—with the help of her family—Tonya has managed to get herself clean of drugs.

At 13 Tonya had her first experience of cocaine. She loved the feeling of excitement and confidence it gave her and began taking it more and more often. Because cocaine is a

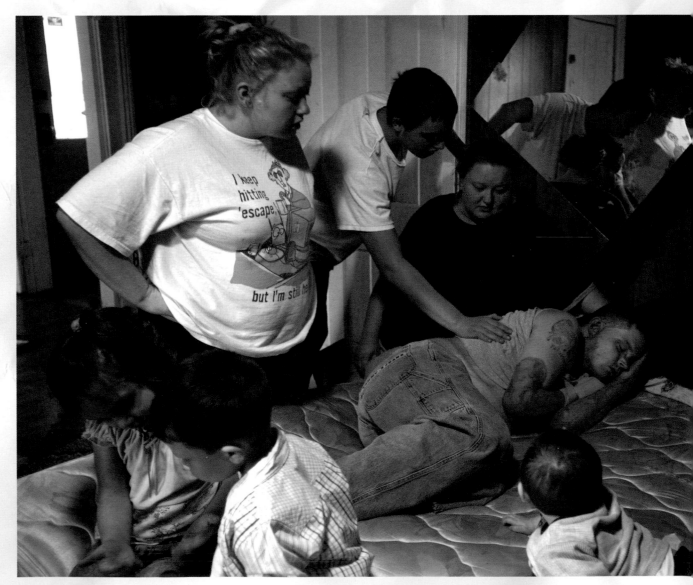

Interventions

An intervention happens when a group of family and friends band together because they are worried about someone. They meet to warn the person that they are concerned and want them to change their behavior before it is too late. The families and friends of alcoholics and drug users use interventions to force them to get treatment for their addictions. Faced with so many people saying that they have a problem and need help with it, drug addicts find it hard to carry on claiming that they are really okay and can cope on their own.

stimulant, the user finds it hard to sleep. Tonya began to sniff heroin at the end of the day: heroin is a depressant, so it made it easier for her to get to sleep. Soon she had a taste for the relaxed feeling heroin gave and she started injecting it.

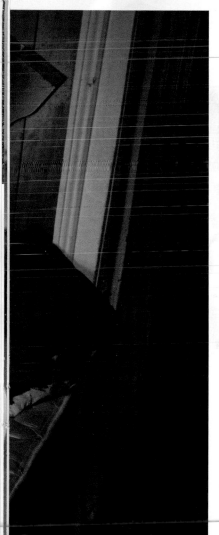

Tonya began to hang out with a new group of friends. They weren't people she especially liked, and she would not have been friends with them a couple of years earlier. The only thing they all had in common was that they were into drugs. Together they would steal and cheat to get money to pay for drugs. Tonya's behavior began to change in other ways. She was irritable, tired all the time, and her grades at school went down. Tonya's mother began to realize there was something wrong.

In the end Tonya's whole family realized she was ruining her life. Tonya's mother, aunts, uncle, older brother, and two favorite cousins came to her house. One by one they each told her that they were worried about her and that they knew she was on drugs. At first Tonya denied it and tried to laugh it off. Her family wouldn't believe her, and in the end she broke down in tears and admitted that she was a heroin addict. Tonya promised to get treatment.

Today Tonya has gotten her life back on track. She has finished high school, and is just about to start college. Best of all, she is happy, healthy, and free of drugs. "I could never have saved myself without the help of my family, especially my mom," she says.

◀ **This young man has been awake for several days while taking drugs. He has fallen asleep and cannot be woken up, so his family watch over him in case he needs medical attention.**